SRA/McGraw-Hill

A Division of The **McGraw-Hill** *Companies*

Copyright © 1997 SRA/McGraw-Hill.

Printed in the United States of America.

Send all inquiries to:
SRA/McGraw-Hill
250 Old Wilson Bridge Road
Suite 310
Worthington, Ohio 43085

ISBN 0-02-687871-2

SRA/McGraw-Hill
Columbus, Ohio

1 2 3 4 5 6 7 8 9 POH 00 99 98 97 96

What is it?

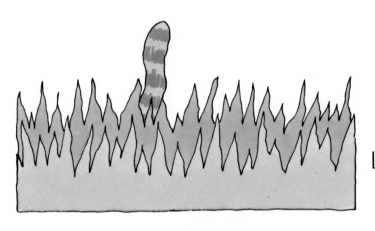

Something is in the grass.
Look at it go.

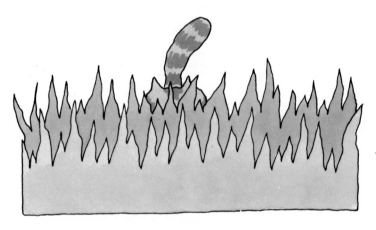

It goes fast in the grass.
Now it is walking near.
What is it?

What is in the grass?
Now I can see it.
It is Mack in the grass.

Picture Interpretation and Guided Reading (For All Stories): Introduce students to Mack, a mischievous cat who is the main character throughout the book. Encourage them to look at the pictures and to tell what is happening. Have them relate what they see to their own experiences. Anticipate the vocabulary needs of the group. Recognition of words in the story may be developed by writing key words on the chalkboard as the pictures are discussed. Let students read the story silently. Help them with words they do not recognize. Then have students read the story orally. The teacher annotations may be used to guide discussion.

1. gr

_____   _____   _____

2. a   e

3. i   u

4. o   u

5. a   e

6. i   o

7. a   u

8.

_____   _____   _____

Up They Go

Mack walks in the grass.
He sees something pretty.
He wants to get it.

Now there are two.
Mack runs here and there.
He jumps and jumps.

Now there are three.
Up and up they go.
They are fast.
Mack cannot get them.

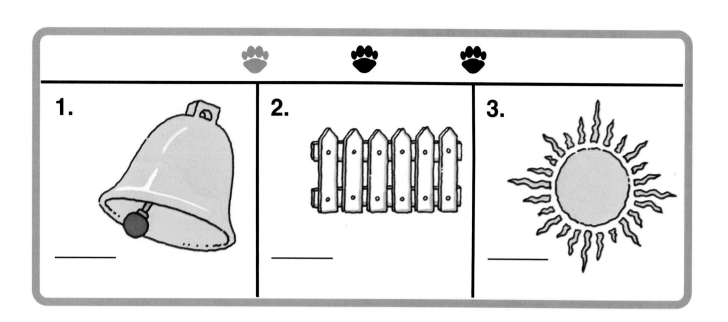

4. pr

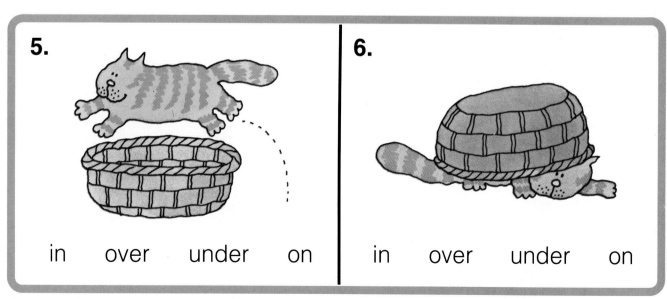

5. in   over   under   on

6. in   over   under   on

5

Fun in the Sun

Mack is playing in the sun.
Something is playing with him.
Mack walks and it walks.

It goes everywhere with Mack.
Mack stops and it stops.
Mack goes faster and faster.
He looks back and there it is!

Mack jumps and it jumps.
Mack runs and it runs.
Mack says, "This is fun."
He likes to play in the sun.

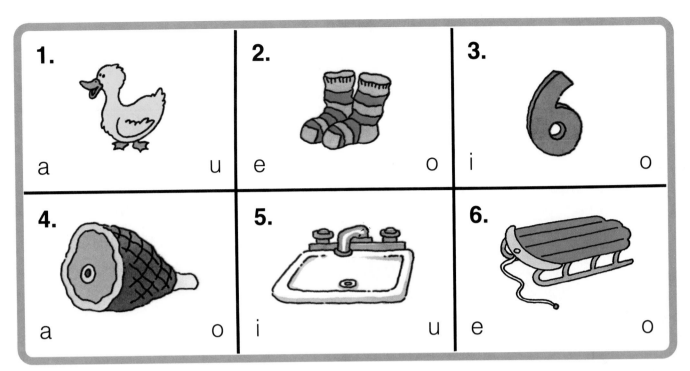

1. a   u

2. e   o

3. i   o

4. a   o

5. i   u

6. e   o

7. sun	Mack
8. back	fun
9. see	tree
10. my	white
11. kite	fly

12. Mack is walking on the _____.

water   grass   sun

13. Mack had _____ playing.

fun   water   toy

Short Vowels (1–6): Have students name each picture and listen to the vowel sound. Have them circle the correct vowel below the picture.
Rhyming Words (7–11): Have students read the words and then draw lines to connect the words that rhyme.
Context Clues (12–13): Have students read each sentence and circle the word that best completes the sentence. Then have them write the word in the blank. **7**

Mack Jumps Back

Mack looked down.
Something was in there.
"What is it?" said Mack.
"I will find out."

It was something little.
Mack saw it look out at him.
He jumped back.

Mack ran fast.
Something looked out.
"What was that?" it said.
"What looked down here?"

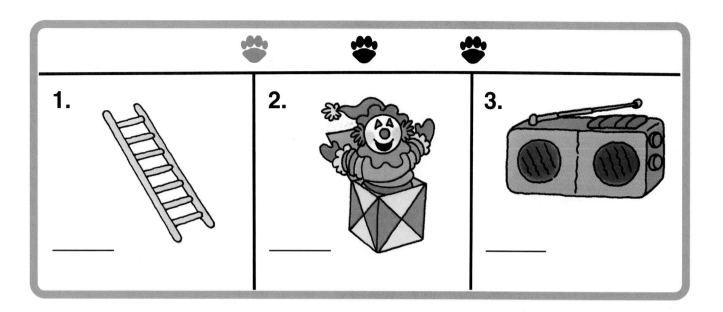

1. _____

2. _____

3. _____

4. _____

5. _____

6. _____

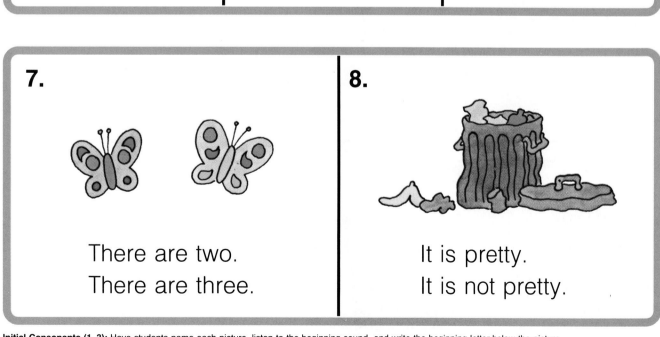

7.

There are two.
There are three.

8.

It is pretty.
It is not pretty.

Initial Consonants (1–3): Have students name each picture, listen to the beginning sound, and write the beginning letter below the picture.
Final Consonants (4–6): Have students name each picture, listen to the ending sound, and write the ending letter below the picture.
Picture Clues (7–8): Direct students to read the sentences in each box and circle the sentence that best describes the picture.

9

The Big Tree

Mack has run and played.
Now he wants to sleep.
His tree is near.

Mack goes to his tree.
It is a big tree.
Mack likes to sleep in it.

Up he goes.
Mack likes this tree.
He likes to sleep up here.

1. _____

2. _____

3. _____

4.   e   o

5.   a   u

6.   i   u

7.   i   o

8.   a   e

9.   o   u

10.

Mack plays in the sun.
He sees something coming.
It cannot go fast.
What is it?

     a squirrel
     a turtle
     a house

11.

Mack plays in the grass.
A turtle comes near.
Mack cannot see it.
Where is the turtle?

     on a ball
     in back of Mack
     under the snow

Initial Consonants (1–3): Have students name each picture, listen to the beginning sound, and write the beginning letter below the picture.
Short Vowels (4–9): Have students name each picture and listen to the vowel sound. Have them circle the correct vowel below the picture.
Drawing Conclusions (10–11): Have students read the sentences in each box. Then have them circle the phrase that makes the most sense.

Mack Plays with Muffin

Mack was in his tree.
He was not sleeping.
Mack could see everywhere.
He saw Muffin near the tree.

Muffin looked and looked.
She had come to find Mack.
She did not see him.

Mack jumped down at Muffin.
Muffin jumped back at Mack.
They had fun playing.

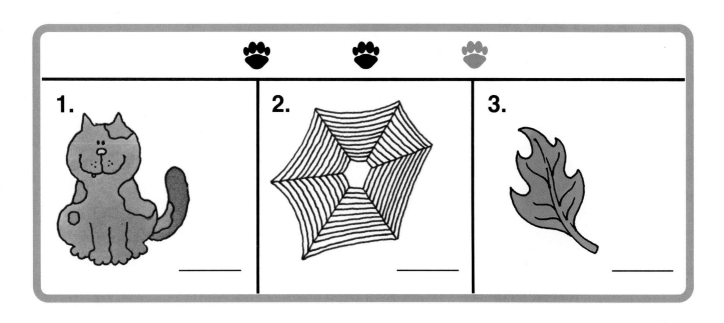

1. _____

2. _____

3. _____

ran	his	three	two

4. is _____

5. can _____

6. she _____

7. you _____

8.
Mack is in the grass.
He wants to play.
Mack will ____.

> look at the grass
> sleep in the sun
> go find Muffin

9.
Mack and Muffin see a ball.
They run to get it.
Muffin runs faster.
____ will get the ball.

> Mack
> Muffin

Final Consonants (1–3): Have students name each picture, listen to the ending sound, and write the ending letter below the picture.
Rhyming Words (4–7): Have students read the words at the top of the box. Then have them read each numbered word. Direct students to find the word at the top that rhymes with the numbered word. Have them write the rhyming word in the blank.
Predicting Outcomes (8–9): Have students read the sentences in each box. Then have them circle the phrase or word below that makes sense.

Up a Tree

Mack saw something in the tree.
"What is up there?" he said.
"I want to see what it is."

Mack ran up the tree.
He saw a nest.
It had three birds in it.
The mother was not home.

The mother came back.
She saw Mack in the tree.
"Go away, Mack!" she said.
"You go home!"

1. qu

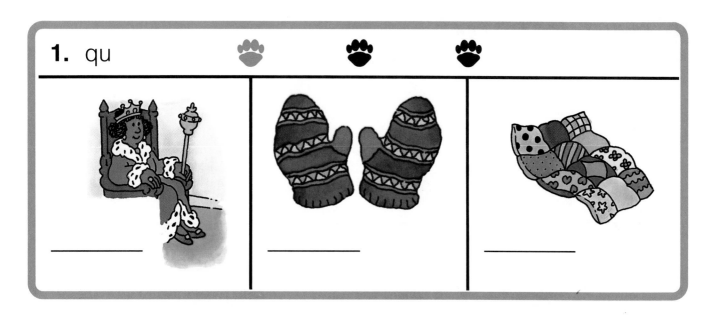

2.   **3.**   **4.**

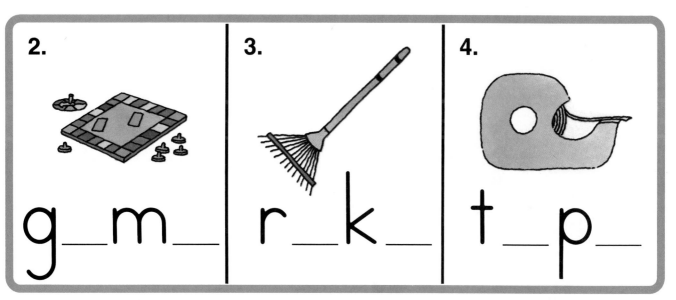

g__m__ | r__k__ | t__p__

5. Mack saw something in the ___.	tree		grass
6. The nest had ___ birds.	two		three
7. The mother was ___ home.	at		not
8. The mother said, "___, Mack!"	Come		Go away

Initial Consonants (1): Review the sound of the letters **qu.** Have students name each picture. Direct them to write **qu** below each picture whose name begins with the **qu** sound. Have them put **X** directly on the picture that does not begin with the **qu** sound.
Long Vowels (2–4): Review the sound of long **a.** Have students name each picture and listen to the vowel sound. Have them write the letters **a** and **e** to complete each picture name.
Facts and Details (5–8): Have students read each sentence and, based on the story events, circle the correct answer.

15

A Big Friend

Mack went for a walk.
He stopped fast.
His back went up.
Something big was there.

Mack looked up at it.
"This is a big dog," he said.
"I will run home fast."

"Do not go," said Muffin.
"I think the dog likes you.
He wants to be a friend."

1. _____

2. _____

3. _____

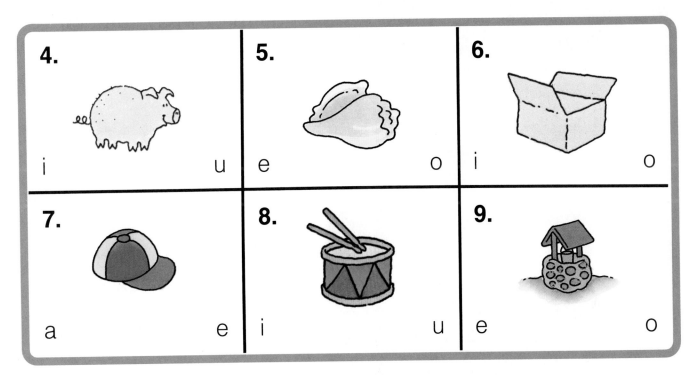

4.   i   u

5.   e   o

6.   i   o

7.   a   e

8.   i   u

9.   e   o

10. A _____ is in the tree.

       nest   dog   doll

11. He is my _____.

       mother   house   friend

Final Consonants (1–3): Have students name each picture, listen to the ending sound, and write the ending letter beside the picture.
Short Vowels (4–9): Have students name each picture and listen to the vowel sound. Have them circle the correct vowel below the picture.
Context Clues (10–11): Have students read each sentence and circle the word that best completes the sentence. Then have them write the word in the blank.

17

Funny Fred

Mack and Muffin like
to run.
They go to the water.
Fred the frog is there.
They think Fred is funny.

Fred jumps up and down.
He jumps down and up.
Muffin jumps into the water
with Fred.

Now the water is on Mack.
"I don't like that," he says.
"The water isn't fun.
I will go to my tree."

1. fr

_____   _____   _____

don't   isn't   can't

2. is not _____

3. do not _____

4. can not _____

5.

The water comes out.

It goes everywhere.

Mack and Muffin run away.

They ___ water.

like   don't like

6.

It is something that jumps.

It likes water.

It can't run fast.

It is a ___.

duck   frog   dog

Blends (1): Review the sound of the blend **fr.** Have students name each picture. Direct them to write **fr** below each picture whose name begins with the **fr** sound. Have them put **X** directly on the picture that does not begin with the **fr** sound.
Contractions (2–4): Explain the concept of contractions to students, and have them read the contractions at the top of the box. Then have them read each numbered pair of words. In the blank, have students write the contraction for the two words.
Drawing Conclusions (5–6): Have students read the sentences in each box. Then have them circle the word or phrase that makes the most sense.

19

Mack Wants Water

Mack wants
some water.
Can he get it here?
Mack looks and looks.
Will the water come out?

Mack looks into it, but
he can't see the water.
Will it come out?

Mack wants some
water, and here
it comes!
The water is
coming down.
Mack can get it now.

1. k _ t _

2. f _ r _

3. b _ k _

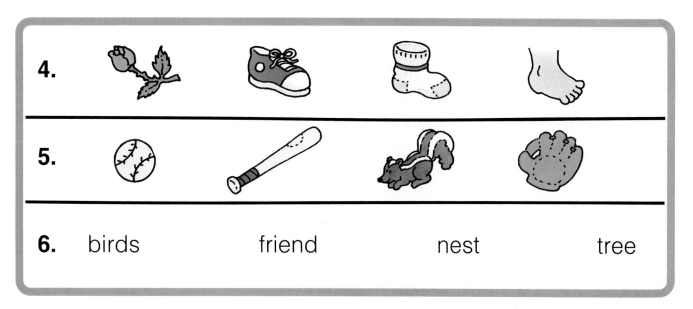

6. birds   friend   nest   tree

7. "Get down, Mack!"
"You are funny, Mack."

8. "Go up there."
"Come down here!"

Long Vowels (1–3): Review the sound of long **i.** Have students name each picture and listen to the vowel sound. Have them write the letters **i** and **e** to complete each picture name.
Classification (4–6): Have students look at all four pictures or words in each row and circle the three that belong together.
Picture Clues (7–8): Direct students to look at the picture and read the sentences in each box. Have them circle the sentence that they would say to Mack.

In the Sun

Mack stopped near
his tree.
The sun was out.
He liked the sun.
It was hot on his back.

The sun went away.
"Where did it go?"
said Mack.
"I am cold when there is no
sun on my back."

The sun came out again.
Mack liked the hot sun on
his back.
He went to sleep in
the sun.

1. _____

2. _____

3. _____

4. g__t___

5. f__v___

6. l__k___

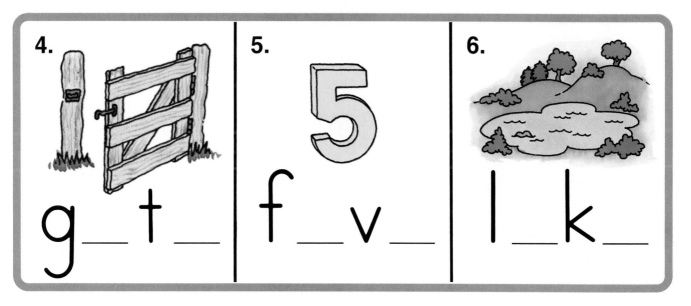

7.

Mack sees something run up a tree.
He wants to see what it is.
What will Mack do?

> play with a friend
> get some hot water
> run up the tree

8.

A frog plays in the sun.
The frog is hot.
What will the frog do?

> jump into cold water
> jump up and down
> sleep in the sun

Final Consonants (1–3): Have students name each picture, listen to the ending sound, and write the ending letter below the picture.
Long Vowels (4–6): Have students name each picture and listen to the vowel sound. Have them write the letters that complete the picture name.
Predicting Outcomes (7–8): Have students read the sentences in each box. Then have them circle the phrase below that makes sense.

23

Look Out, Mack!

Mack was sleeping in his tree.
Something came down.
Mack looked up and saw Zippy.

Mack ran up the tree.
Zippy ran up, too.
Zippy ran out of the tree.

Zippy jumped to the next tree.
Mack wanted to jump, too.
Look out, Mack!
You are too big!

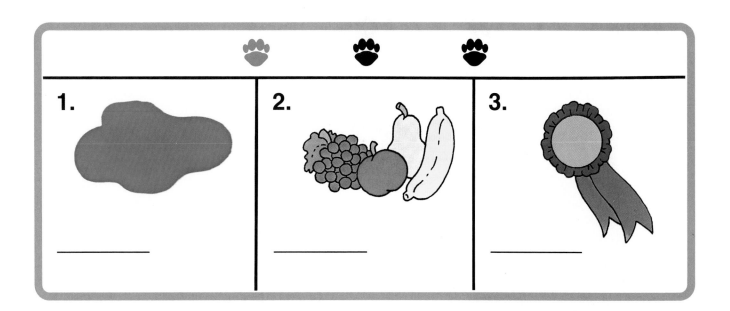

1. _____

2. _____

3. _____

4. wh

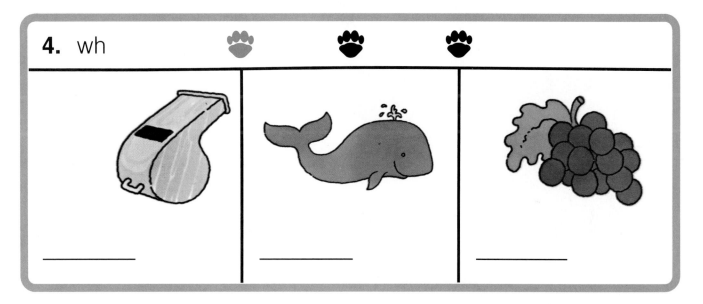

_____ _____ _____

5.	Mack was ___ in his tree.	sleeping	playing
6.	Mack looked ___ and saw Zippy.	down	up
7.	Zippy jumped to the ___.	next tree	grass
8.	Mack was too ___ to jump.	little	big

Blends (1–3): Have students name each picture, listen to the beginning sound, and write the beginning blend below the picture.
Consonant Digraphs (4): Review the sound of the consonant digraph **wh.** Have students name each picture. Direct them to write **wh** below each picture whose name begins with the **wh** sound. Have them put **X** directly on the picture that does not begin with the **wh** sound.
Facts and Details (5–8): Have students read each sentence and, based on the story events, circle the correct answer.

25

Looking for Zippy

This is where Zippy the squirrel lives.
Who is in the tree?
Is that Zippy?

That isn't Zippy
the squirrel.
It is too big to be Zippy.
Who is in her home?

It is Mack!
He is looking for Zippy, but she isn't there.
Get out of that tree, Mack!
You are too big!

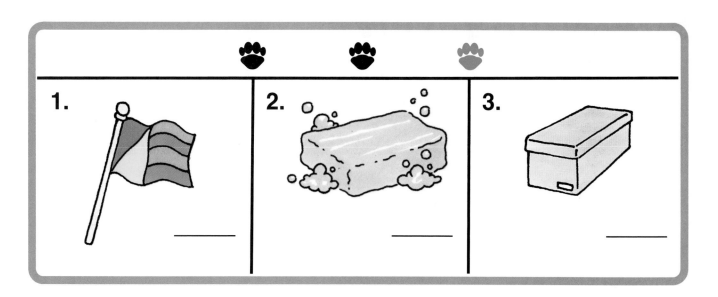

1. _____

2. _____

3. _____

4. r _ s _

5. b _ n _

6. r _ p _

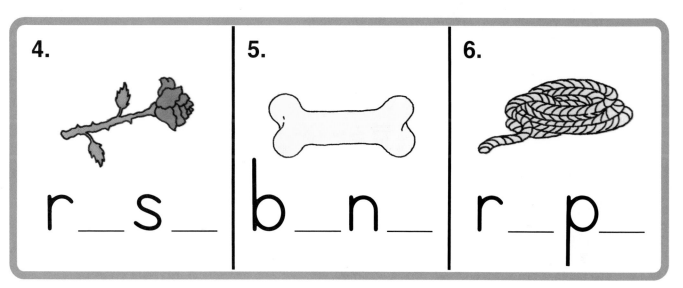

7.

Mack is sleeping.
The sun is on his back.
He rolls over.
Where is Mack?

> on the grass
> in a tree
> in the water

8.

Something is in the tree.
It has birds in it.
What is it?

> a squirrel
> a nest
> a kite

Final Consonents (1–3): Have students name each picture, listen to the ending sound, and write the ending letter below the picture.
Long Vowels (4–6): Review the sound of long **o.** Have students name each picture and listen to the vowel sound. Have them write the letters **o** and **e** to complete each picture name.
Drawing Conclusions (7–8): Have students read the sentences in each box. Then have them circle the phrase that makes the most sense.

Something New

Something was on
the grass.
It was something new.
Mack wanted to see it, so
he went in to look.

Muffin came running.
She wanted to play.
"Here is a string,"
she said.
"I think I can get it."

Muffin did get the string.
The tent came down.
"Meow, meow!"
said Mack.
"I want out!"

1. th

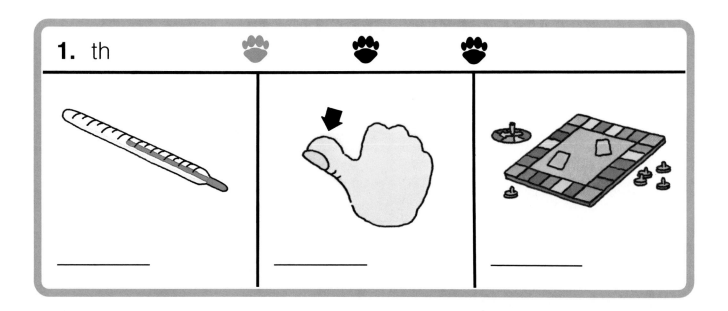

2.

Do you ____ to play?
want   wants   wanted

3.

Mack ____ with a ball.
play   plays   playing

4.

Mack is ____ for Muffin.
looks   looked   looking

5.

The frog has ____.
jumps   jumped   jumping

6.

Consonant Digraphs (1): Review the sound of the consonant digraph **th.** Have students name each picture. Direct them to write **th** below each picture whose name begins with the **th** sound. Have them put **X** directly on the picture that does not begin with the **th** sound.
Base Words and Endings (2–5): Have students read each sentence and circle the word that correctly completes the sentence.
Sequence (6): Have students look at all three pictures. Direct them to write **1** below the event that would happen first, **2** below the event that would happen second, and **3** below the event that would happen third.

29

Mack and the String

Mack sees a kite and a ball of string.
He looks this way and that.
Mack wants to play with the string.

Mack jumps up, but the ball goes down.
It rolls faster and faster.
Mack cannot get the ball.

Mack runs to stop the ball.
The ball rolls and rolls.
Mack rolls, too.
Now look at funny Mack.
The string is all around him.

1. m__l__

2. f__s__

3. c__b__

4. **where**   tent   there   who

5. **hot**   not   her   new

6. **stop**   sun   play   pop

7. **some**   cold   come   said

8. **tent**   them   went   want

9. "Walk here, Mack."
"Don't walk in here."

10. "You can sleep here, Mack."
"You can't sleep here."

Long Vowels (1–3): Review the sound of long **u.** Have students name each picture and listen to the vowel sound. Have them write the letters **u** and **e** to complete each picture name.

Rhyming Words (4–8): Have students read the words in each row. Direct them to circle the word that rhymes with the first word in each row.

Picture Clues (9–10): Direct students to look at the picture and read the sentences in each box. Have them circle the sentence that they would say to Mack.

Something Is Coming

Mack looks up.
"Something is up there,"
he says.
"I will go up to see what it is."

Look out, Mack!
Don't play there!
A bee is coming!
Jump down and run fast!

Mack jumps and runs.
He sees Muffin.
"Run away, Muffin!"
says Mack.
"A big bee is coming.
Run fast!"

Diagnostic Reading Pretest for **Mack**

Possible Total Score: 47

Name _____

Total Score _____

Part A

● d 🐕 p | **1.** 🪺 m n | **2.** 👑 g qu | **3.** 💍 f r

🛑 (STOP) Score _____ Possible Score 3

Part B

● f 🍁 t | **1.** 📦 k x | **2.** 🕸️ b p | **3.** 🐖 c g

🛑 (STOP) Score _____ Possible Score 3

Part C

● fr 🚆 tr | **1.** 🍇 fl gr | **2.** 🎁 pl pr | **3.** 🐸 fl fr

4. 👍 th wh | **5.** 🍒 ch sh | **6.** 👟 ch sh | **7.** 🪈 th wh

🛑 (STOP) Score _____ Possible Score 7

Part D

● a 🎩 e | **1.** i **6** o | **2.** a 🫙 o | **3.** e 🛏️ u

🛑 (STOP) Score _____ Possible Score 3

Part E

• m _ l _

1. r _ k _

2. b _ n _

3. k _ t _

Score _____ Possible Score 3

Part F

sun
near
back
new

• Mack _____

1. here _____

2. fun _____

3. too _____

Score _____ Possible Score 3

Part G

• do not _____

1. is not _____

2. did not _____

3. was not _____

Score _____ Possible Score 3

Part H

• w a l k i n g   **1.** l o o k e d   **2.** j u m p e d   **3.** l i v e s

4. w a n t e d   **5.** e a t i n g   **6.** r o l l e d   **7.** r u n s

Score _____ Possible Score 7

Part I

● must   next
nest

1. sun   some
stay

2. big   both
birds

3. friend   frog
from

Score _____ Possible Score 3

Part J

●

1.

2.

3.

Score _____ Possible Score 3

Part K

Mack played one day.
He rolled in the grass.
He jumped over
the flowers.
Mack saw a pretty flower.
It was little and white.
"I will give it to Muffin,"
Mack said.
"I like Muffin.
She is my friend."

● Mack ___ in the grass.
jumped   walked   rolled

1. Mack jumped over ___.
flowers   birds   spring

2. The flower was ___.
big   cold   white

3. Muffin is Mack's ___.
mother   frog   friend

Score _____ Possible Score 3

Part L

●

Mack ran up a tree.
He saw something up there.
In it was something little.
What did Mack see?

a little white dog
a pretty tent
a nest with a bird

1.

Mack is eating something.
It is a funny thing to eat.
It is pretty and white.
What is Mack eating?

a flower
a tree
some grass

2.

Mack has a good friend.
It lives in a house.
It likes to play ball.
Who is Mack's friend?

Muffin, the dog
Zippy, the squirrel
Fred, the frog

3.

Two birds are in a tree.
A big squirrel comes up.
The birds don't like this.
What will the birds do?

run to a house
fly away
sleep in the nest

STOP

Score _____ Possible Score 3

Part M

●

My friends and I play ___.

tag   game   kite

1.

Mack likes the ___ sun.

cold   tired   hot

2.

His mother ___ home.

can't   don't   isn't

3.

A ball ___ into the grass.

walked   looked   rolled

 STOP

Score _____ Possible Score 3

Diagnostic Reading Posttest for Mack

Possible Total Score: 47

Name _____

Total Score _____

Part A

● b [duck] d | **1.** h [net] n | **2.** qu [quilt] x | **3.** r [radio] p

STOP

Score _____ Possible Score 3

Part B

● f [scarf] k | **1.** x [fox] z | **2.** b [crib] q | **3.** g [frog] k

STOP

Score _____ Possible Score 3

Part C

● pr [truck] tr | **1.** gr [grass] pr | **2.** pl [ribbon] pr | **3.** fr [frame] tr

4. th [thermometer] wh | **5.** ch [cheese] sh | **6.** ch [shirt] sh | **7.** th [wheel] wh

STOP

Score _____ Possible Score 7

Part D

● a [bat] o | **1.** i [pig] u | **2.** e [sock] o | **3.** a [sled] e

STOP

Score _____ Possible Score 3

Posttest Page 1

Part E

● c _ b _

1. c _ n _

2. r _ s _

3. f _ r _

Score _____ Possible Score 3

Part F

ran
me
come
snow

● some _____

1. three _____

2. go _____

3. can _____

STOP

Score _____ Possible Score 3

Part G

● was not _____

1. did not _____

2. is not _____

3. do not _____

STOP

Score _____ Possible Score 3

Part H

● w a l k e d 1. s t a y i n g 2. r o l l e d 3. e a t i n g
4. f i n d s 5. l o o k e d 6. w a n t s 7. p l a y e d

STOP

Score _____ Possible Score 7

Part I

● game   good
grass

1. be   bee
back

2. don't   day
dog

3. friends   from
flower

Score _____ Possible Score 3

Part J

●

1.

2.

3.

Score _____ Possible Score 3

Part K

Mack walked in the sun.
He went near the water and
saw something.
"What is it?" said Mack.
All at once, it jumped.
Then there was water
on Mack.
"Now I see," he said.
"It is my friend the frog."

● Mack went near the ___.
flowers   tree   water

1. Mack saw something ___.
jump   fly   pop

2. There was ___ on Mack.
string   snow   water

3. A ___ had jumped.
rabbit   frog   duck

Score _____ Possible Score 3

●
A bird is in the grass.
It wants to be in the nest.
It can't fly to the nest.
It is too __ to fly.

> big
> little
> happy

1.
Mack ran around the house.
He ran up and down a tree.
Then Mack was __, so he stopped running.

> tired
> pretty
> cold

2.
Muffin rolled something to Mack.
Mack rolled it back.
What were they doing?

> playing with a ball
> playing tag
> playing with a doll

3.
Mack sees some flowers.
He wants to eat them.
A bee is in the flowers.
What will Mack do?

> run at the bee
> go away
> eat the flowers

STOP

Score _____ Possible Score 3

●
A __ is on the flower.

> bee   frog   nest

1.
Rabbit __ over a flower.

> wanted   jumped   liked

2.
Flowers are __ the house.

> under   over   around

3.
__ lives in that house?

> When   Who   Where

Score _____ Possible Score 3

1. _____ go near that bee.
(Do not)

2. Her friend _____ home.
(is not)

isn't
can't
don't

3.
(look)s
looked
looking

_____

4.
jumps
jumped
jumping

_____

5.
wants
wanted
wanting

_____

6. A _____ likes to play in water.
frog   squirrel   bee

7. When a _____ comes near, Mack runs.
friend   mother   bee

Contractions (1–2): Have students read each sentence with the two words below the blank. Then have them read the contractions in the box and write the correct one in each blank. Tell students that one of the three contractions in the box will not be used.
Base Words and Endings (3–5): Have students read the words in each box. Direct their attention to the circled word **look,** and explain the concept of base words. Have students circle the base words in each box and then write the base word in the blank.
Context Clues (6–7): Have students read each sentence and circle the word that best completes the sentence. Then have them write the word in the blank.

33

Big and White

Mack was in his tree.
He saw something pretty
and white.
"That is a turtle.
It is a big white turtle,"
he said.

"Now I see a duck.
It is walking.
A big white duck is walking.
It wants to get that ball."

"Now what is that?"
Mack said.
"It looks like Zippy
the squirrel.
Come down here, Zippy.
I want to play with you."

1. _____

2. _____

3. _____

4. h__s__

5. m__l__

6. r__b__

7. This is a home for Zippy.
This is a home for birds.

8. It is hot out there.
It is cold out there.

Consonant Digraphs (1–3): Have students name each picture, listen to the beginning sound, and write the beginning consonant digraph in the blank below the picture.
Long Vowels (4–6): Have students name each picture and listen to the vowel sound. Have them write the letters that complete the picture name.
Picture Clues (7–8): Direct students to read the sentences in each box and circle the sentence that best describes the picture.

35

In the Flowers

Mack was in the flowers.
Muffin likes to come
here, too.
Mack looked for Muffin,
but she was not around.

Mack did not jump
or walk.
He did not run or play.
He just looked for Muffin.
"Here she comes,"
Mack said.

Muffin came near
the flowers.
Mack jumped out very fast.
He jumped on Muffin.
"Here I am!" said Mack.
"You are funny,"
said Muffin.

1. _____

2. _____

3. _____

4.

5. flower　　　　mother　　　　tree　　　　grass

6. not　　　　isn't　　　　can't　　　　don't

7. _____　　　_____　　　_____

Blends (1–3): Have students name each picture, listen to the beginning sound, and write the beginning blends below the picture.
Classification (4–6): Have students look at all four pictures or words in each row and circle the three that belong together.
Sequence: (7): Have students look at all three pictures. Direct them to write **1** below the event that would happen first, **2** below the event that would happen second, and **3** below the event that would happen third.

37

Mack Runs

Mack likes to run. Sometimes he goes up the tree and comes down running. He runs around in the grass. Then he goes back up the tree and runs down again. Mack runs everywhere.

Muffin likes to run, too. Sometimes she runs with Mack. They jump and run and play tag. They go faster and faster.

Mack and Muffin have stopped running. They are tired and want to sleep. Sometimes they just sleep and sleep.

1. sh

_____

_____

_____

2.

Mack has _____ running.

stop   stops   stopped

3.

A squirrel _____ down the tree.

come   comes   coming

4.

Muffin is _____ very fast.

run   runs   running

5.

I don't _____ that bee.

like   likes   liked

6.

Muffin jumps and plays.
She runs fast.
She gets tired.
What will she do next?

    run faster

    play tag

    go to sleep

7.

Mack and Muffin are playing.
A bee is coming.   It is
something they do not like.
What will they do next?

    run away

    play with the bee

    run at the bee

Consonant Digraphs (1): Review the sound of the consonant digraph **sh.** Have students name each picture. Direct them to write **sh** below each picture whose name begins with the **sh** sound. Have them put **X** directly on the picture that does not begin with the **sh** sound.
Base Words and Endings (2–5): Have students read each sentence and circle the word that correctly completes the sentence.
Predicting Outcomes (6–7): Have students read the sentences in each box. Then have them circle the phrase below that makes sense.

Mack Likes Flowers

Mack likes pretty flowers. "I think I will eat this one," he said. "Yes, it is a good flower. I like it."

"Now I will try a new one," said Mack. "This one is pretty. But it isn't very good. I do not like it."

Mack did not stop eating. He went from flower to flower. "It is fun to try them," he said. "I like eating pretty flowers."

1. _____

2. _____

3. _____

4. Where is Mack?

H____ is in his tree.

5. Where is Muffin?

Sh____ is not here.

6.

They are good to play with.
You cannot play with them.

7.

They are good to walk on.
Do not walk on them.

Blends (1–3): Have students name each picture, listen to the beginning sound, and write the beginning blend in the blank below the picture.
Long Vowels (4–5): Review the sound of long **e.** Have students read each item and decide what the incomplete word should be. Have them write the letter **e** to complete the word.
Picture Clues (6–7): Direct students to read the sentences in each box and circle the sentence that best describes the picture.

Look at Me

"One, two, three, look at me. I will run and have some fun," said Mack. "I will jump over the flowers, too. Meow! Look at me!"

Mack rolled over and over. He played in the grass and ran in the flowers. Mack was very happy.

The sun was everywhere. Mack liked the pretty day. "Three, two, one, this is fun," he said. "What a day to run and play. Look at me!"

1.	a		u
2.	e		u
3.	i		o
4.	e		o
5.	a		i
6.	o		u

7.	eating	jumping	walking	running
8.	three	one	happy	two
9.	to	too	three	two

10. Here is a _____ flower.
           tired   pretty   fast

11. I _____ tag with my friend.
rolled   stopped   played

Short Vowels (1–6): Have students name each picture and listen to the vowel sound. Have them circle the correct vowel below the picture.
Classification (7–9): Have students read all four words in each row and circle the three that belong together.
Context Clues (10–11): Have students read each sentence and circle the word that best completes the sentence. Then have them write the word in the blank.

43

A Funny Flower

Mack saw a white flower in the grass. "The flower is pretty," said Mack. He ran to look at it.

Mack ran into the flower. "Look at that!" he said. Some of the flower went up. Some of it went down. Some of it went this way, and some went that way. The flower went everywhere.

"It isn't like other flowers," said Mack. "It is a funny flower. I will try to tag it. It is fun to see it go."

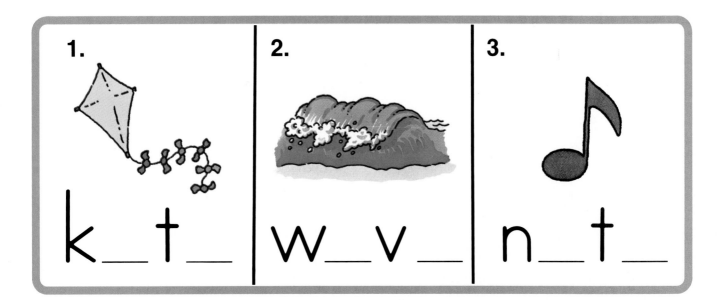

1. k __ t __

2. w __ v __

3. n __ t __

---

other   bee   try   day

4. fly _____

5. play _____

6. mother _____

7. tree _____

---

8. A ____ flower was in the grass.	cold	white
9. Mack ____ into the flower.	ran	walked
10. The flower went ____ .	everywhere	down
11. Mack wanted to ____ the flower.	eat	tag

Long Vowels (1–3): Have students name each picture and listen to the vowel sound. Have them write the letters that complete the picture name.
Rhyming Words (4–7): Have students read the words at the top of the box. Then have them read each numbered word. Direct students to find the word at the top that rhymes with the numbered word. Have them write the rhyming word in the blank.
Facts and Details (8–11): Have students read each sentence and, based on the story events, circle the correct answer.

I See You

Mack and Muffin were playing. "You go," said Mack. "I will stay here. Then I will try to find you."

Muffin ran and ran. She stopped in the flowers. "I will stay in here," she said. "Mack cannot see me in the flowers."

Mack looked for Muffin. He walked near the flowers. He saw Muffin, but he didn't want her to know. Mack walked on by and then stopped. All at once he jumped on Muffin. "Meow!" Mack said. "I see you!"

1. ch

_____   _____   _____

2.

p l a y s
p l a y e d
p l a y i n g

_____

3.

w a l k s
w a l k e d
w a l k i n g

_____

4.

r o l l s
r o l l e d
r o l l i n g

_____

5.

It is little.
It can fly.
It is not good to play with.
What is it?

  a kite
  a bee
  a flower

6.

Zippy runs fast.
Muffin runs fast.
Mack runs to get them.
What are they doing?

  playing tag
  eating flowers
  looking for birds

Consonant Digraphs (1): Review the sound of the consonant digraph **ch.** Have students name each picture. Direct them to write **ch** below each picture whose name begins with the **ch** sound. Have them put **X** directly on the picture that does not begin with the **ch** sound.
Base Words and Endings (2–4): Have students read the words in each box, circle the base words, and write the base word in the blank.
Drawing Conclusions (5–6): Have students read the sentences in each box. Then have them circle the phrase that makes the most sense.

47

Staying In

Mack wanted to go out. But it wasn't a pretty day. "Staying in is not fun," he said. Mack wasn't happy. Then he saw something. "I can play with this," he said.

He made it go this way and that. "I like this game," Mack said. All at once it went up. It went up fast, and Mack jumped down fast.

Mack jumped onto something, and it went down. Things went everywhere. "This is not my day," said Mack.

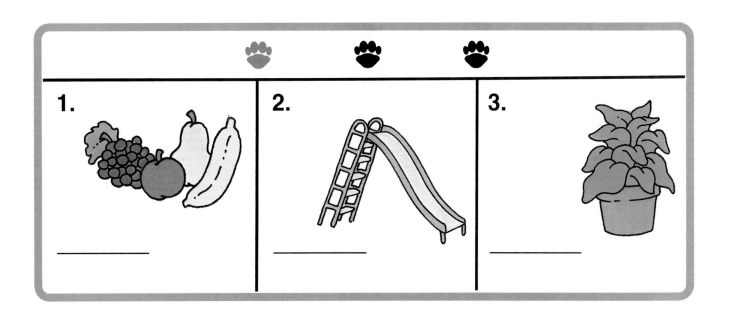

1. _____

2. _____

3. _____

4. do not _____   **5.** was not _____

6. is not _____   **7.** did not _____

8.

_____   _____   _____

Blends (1–3): Have students name each picture, listen to the beginning sound, and write the beginning blend below the picture.
Contractions (4–7): Have students read the two words beside each blank. In the blank, have students write the contraction for the words.
Sequence (8): Have students look at all three pictures. Direct them to write **1** below the event that would happen first, **2** below the event that would happen second, and **3** below the event that would happen third.

A Game with Rabbit

It was a pretty day. Mack and Muffin were walking. Muffin stopped and said, "Who is that?"

"It is Rabbit," said Mack. "Do you want to play with us, Rabbit? We can play a game."

"Yes," said Rabbit. "That will be fun."

So Mack jumped over Muffin. Then he jumped over Rabbit. Muffin jumped over Rabbit. Then she jumped over Mack. Then Rabbit jumped over both of them at once! It was fun, and Rabbit was very good at it.

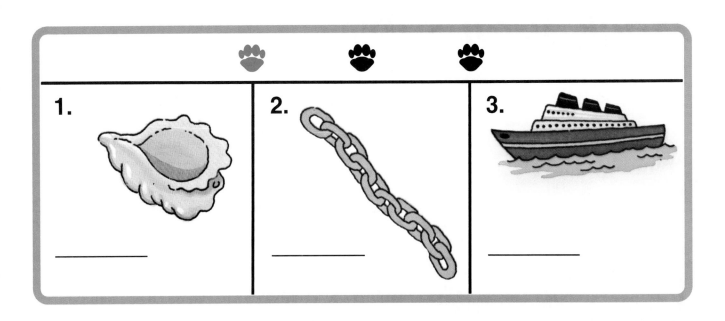

1. _____

2. _____

3. _____

4. f__ s__

5. n__ n__

6. c__ n__

7. Mack and Muffin were ____ .	running	walking
8. Mack and Muffin saw ____.	Rabbit	Zippy
9. They played a ____game.	jumping	running
10. ____was very good at the game.	Rabbit	Muffin

Consonant Digraphs (1–3): Have students name each picture, listen to the beginning sound, and write the beginning consonant digraph in the blank below the picture.
Long Vowels (4–6): Have students name each picture and listen to the vowel sound. Have them write the letters that complete the picture name.
Facts and Details (7–10): Have students read each sentence and, based on the story events, circle the correct answer.

51

Mack Jumps In

Mack found something. "It must be a toy," he said. "It must be for me from Muffin. I can play a game with it."

Mack walked around the thing. He walked one way and then the other. Next Mack ran at it. He ran fast, and he jumped over it. Then Mack said, "I can jump into it. That will be fun!"

Mack ran fast, and he jumped hard. All at once the thing went pop! "This is not my kind of toy," said Mack. "I think I will give it back."

1. The mother bird _____ in her nest.
was not

2. The sun _____ come out all day.
did not

3. flower   rabbit   frog   dog

4. game   doll   birds   kite

5. over   under   on   white

6.
A little snow is on the grass.
The hot sun comes out.
What will the snow do?

     go away
     get very hard
     stay cold and white

7.
Mack wants to give Muffin something.
He wants it to be pretty.
What will Mack give Muffin?

     a bee
     some water
     a flower

Contractions (1–2): Have students read each sentence with the two words below the blank. In the blank, have students write the contraction for the words.
Classification (3–5): Have students read all four words in each row and circle the three that belong together.
Predicting Outcomes (6–7): Have students read the sentences in each box. Then have them circle the phrase below that makes sense.

53

Sounds You Know

1. ___ ___

2. ___ ___

3. ___ ___

4. ___ ___

5. ___ ___

6. ___ ___

7. ___ ___

8. ___ ___

9. ___ ___

10. ___ ___

Initial and Final Consonants, Blends, and Digraphs (1–10): Have students name each picture and listen to the beginning and ending sounds. Direct them to write the letters that stand for the beginning and ending sounds of each picture name in the appropriate blanks.

54

Words You Know

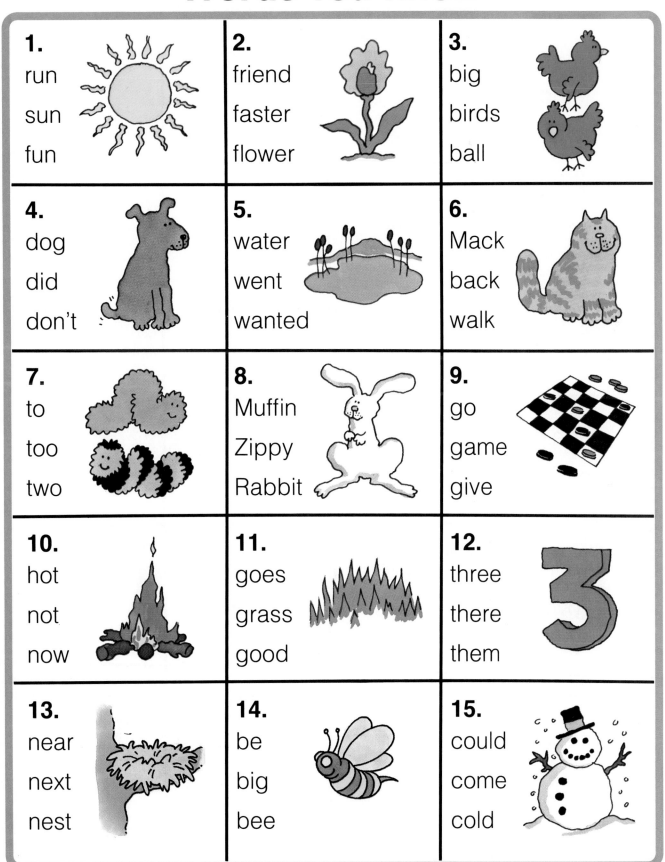

1.
run
sun
fun

2.
friend
faster
flower

3.
big
birds
ball

4.
dog
did
don't

5.
water
went
wanted

6.
Mack
back
walk

7.
to
too
two

8.
Muffin
Zippy
Rabbit

9.
go
game
give

10.
hot
not
now

11.
goes
grass
good

12.
three
there
them

13.
near
next
nest

14.
be
big
bee

15.
could
come
cold

Word Recognition (1–15): Students who have completed all the stories and exercises in *Mack* should be able to recognize and understand the words on this page. Have students name each picture and circle the word that names or best describes the picture.

Words You Know

1. stay stop string	**2.** they them there	**3.** was saw now	**4.** liked likes like
5. walked wanted water	**6.** my by try	**7.** he her here	**8.** friend faster flower
9. away again around	**10.** lives likes looks	**11.** way try play	**12.** thing think this
13. one over other	**14.** have happy has	**15.** some come came	**16.** near new next
17. comes coming some	**18.** must made mother	**19.** frog for from	**20.** just fast nest

Sight Vocabulary (1–20): Students who have completed all the stories and exercises in *Mack* should be able to recognize and understand the words on this page. Direct students to circle the word in each box that you read aloud. Suggested words to pronounce are circled in the Teacher Edition. You may prefer to choose different words to fit the needs of your students.